MW01230531

Dedication

Perspective

Check out these other books by Eric T. Williams on Amazon:

Dedication

This book is dedicated to the remarkable individuals who have been my pillars of support during the most challenging phase of my life. Gigi, Dreka, Torend, B. Cody, and Ahipo, your unwavering words of encouragement, profound wisdom, and genuine love have helped me navigate through moments of immense hardship. With heartfelt gratitude, I thank you for standing by my side when I lost my brother Nate, and my mom Joy. Amidst the multitude of losses I endured during that season, you never faltered in your presence and care. When I felt as though I was on the verge of losing my sanity, you were there, offering me hope and speaking life into my soul.

Your prayers and unwavering support have provided me with strength and solace during those seemingly unbearable times. Your dedication to assist me in every conceivable way will forever remain etched in my heart. As I share this book, " The Power of Kingdom Thinking," with world, it is my fervent prayer that each of you will find abundant blessings in its pages. May you continue your tireless pursuit and work in the Kingdom, spreading the boundless love and grace bestowed upon you by Christ.

Thank you, from the depths of my soul, for being the lamps of the Lord in my life.

With love and appreciation....... Eric T. Williams

Chapter 1: The Fall of Kingdom
Thinking in Adam

In the vast expanse of eternity past, before the foundations of the world were laid, God, in His infinite wisdom and immeasurable love, had a grand plan for His creation. With meticulous detail, He crafted a perfect paradise known as the Garden of Eden, where He placed the pinnacle of His creation, Adam.

Adam, created in the very image and likeness of God, possessed a unique and intimate relationship with the Creator. He was not merely a man, but a beloved son of God, enjoying the blessings and privileges that came with his sonship. In this state of sonship, Adam's mind was aligned with the thoughts and purposes of God, for he possessed what we call "Kingdom thinking."

But alas, tragedy struck when Adam, enticed by the deceitful whispers of the serpent, succumbed to temptation and disobeyed the one command God had given him. In that moment, the blessing of sonship that Adam once enjoyed was lost, and humanity was thrust into a state of brokenness and separation from God. Adam, instead of remaining a son, had become a man of sin, alienated from the very source of life and love.

The loss of Kingdom thinking in Adam reverberated throughout the course of human history. No longer did humanity view life through the lens of their identity as sons and daughters of God. Instead, a new mindset emerged, a mindset driven by self-centeredness, pride, and rebellion against the rightful rule of God.

The impact of this loss was far-reaching, affecting every aspect of human existence. It distorted our understanding of identity, purpose, and relationships. Instead of embracing our role as beloved children of God, we became consumed with our own desires and ambitions, seeking to establish our own kingdoms rather than submitting to the authority of the one true King.

This shift in thinking led to a myriad of consequences. We became enslaved to sin, our hearts and minds clouded by darkness. The harmony that once existed between humanity and creation was shattered, as thorns and thistles sprouted from the ground, and pain and toil became our constant companions. Death entered the world, casting its shadow over every living being.

Yet, even in the midst of this profound loss, God, in His infinite mercy and grace, did not abandon humanity. From the very moment of Adam's transgression, He set in motion a plan of redemption, a plan to restore sonship and Kingdom thinking to His people. This plan culminated in the sending of His only begotten Son, Jesus Christ, to the earth. Jesus, the perfect representation of God's love and Kingdom thinking, came to restore what was lost in Adam.

Through His life, death, and resurrection, Jesus paved the way for all who believe in Him to once again become sons and daughters of God. In Him, the curse of sin was broken, and the power of darkness was defeated. Through faith in Jesus, we are reconciled to our Heavenly Father, adopted into His family, and restored to the fullness of our sonship.

With this glorious truth, a new chapter begins. As we embrace our identity as sons and daughters of God, we are invited to renew our minds and reclaim Kingdom thinking. We are called to align our thoughts, desires, and actions with the principles and purposes of God's Kingdom. Through the power of the Holy Spirit, we can walk in the footsteps of Jesus, reflecting His love, grace, and truth to a broken and hurting world.

Let us, then, cast off the remnants of the man of sin that we inherited from Adam and embrace the glorious reality of our sonship with God. May our lives radiate the light of Kingdom thinking, transforming our families, communities, and nations. And as we journey forward, let us never forget the profound truth that in Christ, we are not only restored sons and daughters, but we are also co-heirs with Him, destined for an eternity of joy and intimate fellowship with our Heavenly Father.

In the words of the Apostle Paul, "For all who are led by the Spirit of God are sons of God. For you did not receive the spirit of slavery to fall back into fear, but you have received the Spirit of adoption as sons, by whom we cry, 'Abba! Father!'" (Romans 8:14-15). May this truth resound within our hearts and guide us as we reclaim the mentality that was lost in Adam, and walk in the fullness of our sonship with God full of the power of Kingdom Thinking.

Kingdom Meditation:

1. Luke 3:38 - "the son of Enos, the son of Seth, the son of Adam, the son of God." This verse acknowledges Adam's position as a son of God.

2. Genesis 1:26-27 - "Then God said, 'Let us make mankind in our image, in our likeness... So God created mankind in his own image, in the image of God he created them; male and female he created them.'" This passage highlights that Adam was created in the image and likeness of God.

3. Romans 5:12 - "Therefore, just as sin entered the world through one man, and death through sin, and in this way death came to all people, because all sinned." This verse speaks of the consequences

of Adam's sin, impacting all of humanity.

4. Romans 8:14-15 - "For all who are led by the Spirit of God are sons of God. For you did not receive the spirit of slavery to fall back into fear, but you have received the Spirit of adoption as sons, by whom we cry, 'Abba! Father!'" This passage emphasizes our adoption as sons and daughters of God through the Spirit.

5. Galatians 4:4-7 - "But when the set time had fully come, God sent his Son, born of a woman, born under the law, to redeem those under the law, that we might receive adoption to sonship. Because you are his sons, God sent the Spirit of his Son into our hearts, the Spirit who calls out, 'Abba, Father.' So you are no longer a slave, but God's child; and since you are his child, God has made you also an heir." This passage speaks of Jesus' redemption and our adoption as children of God.

Chapter 2: The Heavenly
Way of Thinking

In the realm of Kingdom thinking, we delve into the extraordinary nature of Adam, a son of God who possessed a unique connection with heavenly places. Let us embark on a journey to understand the magnificent power of Adam's mind, situated in the realm of the divine, while his physical being resided on the earthly plane.

It has long been postulated that humanity utilizes only a mere 10% of the brain's capacity. However, in the pristine Garden of Eden, before the unfortunate fall from grace, Adam's thoughts were intricately linked with heavenly realms. This profound connection allowed the mind of heaven to manifest on earth, as exemplified by Jesus when he said, "Not my will, but thy will be done on earth, as it is in heaven."

In this state of divine alignment, Adam possessed a deep understanding of his role as the image of God. He saw himself as a spiritual being, created in the likeness of his Heavenly Father. With this heavenly mindset, he was able to perceive the world and all its inhabitants through the lens of divine wisdom. This is how Adam knew what to name each creature, for his mind was attuned to the heavenly understanding of all things on earth.

However, tragically, after partaking of the forbidden fruit from the tree of the knowledge of good and evil, Adam's perception of himself and the world around him drastically changed. No longer did he see himself as the image of God, but rather, he saw himself as mere flesh. As the apostle Paul eloquently put it, Adam became carnally minded instead of spiritually minded. This shift in mindset severed his direct connection with the heavenly realms, clouding his understanding and perception.

The consequences of this fall from grace still reverberate through humanity to this day. We, as descendants of Adam, struggle with the limitations of our carnal minds, often disconnected from the divine wisdom that once flowed through us. Our thoughts are tainted by the influences of the world, and we lose sight of our true identity as sons and daughters of the King.

In our pursuit of the power of Kingdom thinking, it becomes imperative to recognize the significance of restoring our heavenly perspective. We must seek to shed the carnal mindset and realign ourselves with the mind of Christ. This restoration is not a simple task, as it requires a deliberate and conscious effort to overcome the limitations imposed upon us by the fall.

In the subsequent chapters, we shall explore the steps to restore our heavenly mindset, reestablishing our connection with the divine realms. We will uncover the keys to unlocking the full potential of our minds, transcending the limitations of the carnal and embracing the limitless possibilities of the Kingdom.

Remember, dear reader, you were created to be a vessel of divine wisdom, an image-bearer of the Most High. The power to transform your thinking lies within you, waiting to be awakened. As we embark on this journey together, let us cast off the shackles of the carnal mind and embrace the glorious truth that we are spiritual beings, intricately woven into the fabric of eternity.

Prepare yourself, for the revelation of the heavenly way of thinking awaits. And as we walk this path, may our minds be renewed, our spirits rejuvenated, and our lives transformed. The time has come to reclaim our rightful place as sons and daughters of the King, walking in the fullness of our divine inheritance.

So, let us press on, with hearts aflame and minds open to the wonders that await us. The journey towards Kingdom thinking begins now.

Kingdom Meditation:

1. Genesis 1:27 (NIV): "So God created mankind in his own image, in the image of God he created them; male and female he created them."

2. Romans 8:5-6 (NIV): "Those who live according to the flesh have their minds set on what the flesh desires; but those who live in accordance with the Spirit have their minds set on what the Spirit desires. The mind governed by the flesh is death, but the mind governed by the Spirit is life and peace."

3. Colossians 3:2 (NIV): "Set your minds on things above, not on earthly things."

4. Philippians 4:8 (NIV): "Finally, brothers and sisters, whatever is true, whatever is noble, whatever is right, whatever is pure, whatever is lovely, whatever is admirable—if anything is excellent or praiseworthy—think about such things."

5. 2 Corinthians 10:5 (NIV): "We demolish arguments and every pretension that sets itself up against the knowledge of God, and we take captive every thought to make it obedient to Christ."

Chapter 3: The Transformational Process of Restoring Kingdom Thinking

In this chapter, we shall delve into the profound process through which Christ restores believers to a Kingdom mindset, igniting a powerful transformation in their lives. It is important to understand that every aspect of the crucifixion of Christ plays a significant role in restoring us to a proper relationship with the kingdom. However, it is the emblematic crown of thorns that directly addresses our thought process, revealing that Christ has dominion over the cursed way of thinking that plagues humanity. Through His sacrifice, He has bestowed upon us crowns of glory, symbolizing a new way of thinking in alignment with His divine will.

In the book of 1 Peter 5:4, the concept of a crown of glory is introduced, highlighting a fundamental difference between the crown of thorns and the crown of glory. The crown of thorns represents a cursed way of thinking, born from the thorns that emerged as a consequence of the Earth's curse due to the fall of man. However, Jesus, in His infinite love and grace, willingly bore that curse so that we might be reinstated as the beloved sons and daughters of God, equipped with the mind of heaven to exercise dominion on Earth.

To fully grasp the significance of this transformational process, we must first explore the nature of the crown of thorns. The thorns, intrinsically connected to the curse, serve as a painful reminder of the fallen state of humanity. They represent the distorted and destructive thoughts that have plagued mankind since the beginning. But in His redemptive act, Christ took upon Himself the weight of these thorns, thereby breaking their power over us.

By wearing the crown of thorns, Christ not only demonstrated His dominion over the cursed way of thinking, but also revealed His willingness to bear the consequences of humanity's sin. In doing so, He displayed His unrivaled love and desire to restore us to our true identity as children of God. Through His sacrifice, Christ has provided us with the opportunity to shed our old thought patterns and embrace the renewed mindset of the Kingdom.

The crown of glory, on the other hand, represents the Christ way of thinking. It signifies the transformative power of aligning our thoughts with the divine will of God. This crown is not one of pain and suffering, but rather one of honor and victory. It is a crown that illuminates our minds, enabling us to perceive the world through the lens of God's truth and promises.

As we embrace the restoration of our Kingdom thinking, we step into a realm of limitless possibilities. The crown of thorns is no longer our burden to bear; it has been replaced by the crown of glory, which empowers us to walk in the authority and dominion that Christ has bestowed upon us. Through this transformative process, we are elevated to a higher level of thinking, where our minds are aligned with the mind of heaven.

Now, dear reader, I invite you to reflect upon your own thought process. Are you still carrying the weight of the crown of thorns, allowing a cursed way of thinking to dictate your beliefs and actions? Or have you embraced the crown of glory, allowing the Christ way of thinking to shape your worldview?

In this introspective moment, consider the power that lies within your thoughts. Are they aligned with the principles of God's Kingdom, or are they hindered by the thorns of doubt, fear, and negativity?

Remember, the transformational process of restoring Kingdom thinking begins with a conscious decision to surrender our old thought patterns and embrace the mind of Christ. So, my friend, I challenge you to take hold of the crown of glory and allow it to guide your thoughts, for in doing so, you will experience a profound shift in your life, unlocking the power of Kingdom thinking.

Kingdom Meditation:

1. Matthew 6:33 (NIV):
"But seek first his kingdom and his righteousness, and all these things will be given to you as well."

2. Romans 14:17 (NIV):
"For the kingdom of God is not a matter of eating and drinking, but of righteousness, peace and joy in the Holy Spirit."

3. Luke 17:20-21 (NIV):
"Once, on being asked by the Pharisees when the kingdom of God would come, Jesus replied, 'The coming of the kingdom of God is not something that can be observed, nor will people say, 'Here it is,' or 'There it is,' because the kingdom of God is in your midst.'"

Chapter 4: Embracing the Mind of Christ: The Foundation of Kingdom Thinking

Imagine standing next to the towering Empire State Building, marveling at its grandeur and feeling overwhelmed by its sheer size. The immense structure looms above you, leaving you in awe of its magnitude. Yet, as you step into an airplane and soar high above the city, the Empire State Building appears minuscule compared to the vast expanse that stretches out before you. From this heavenly perspective, you grasp the true essence of Kingdom thinking.

In this chapter, we are exploring the concept of embracing the mind of Christ which is Kingdom thinking. This mindset shapes our thoughts, attitudes, and actions, elevating our perception to a higher realm. Just as viewing the Empire State Building from an airplane provides a new perspective, Kingdom thinking allows us to see life from a heavenly vantage point, where the once overwhelming becomes manageable.

The mind of Christ serves as our compass, guiding us through the complexities of life. When we align ourselves with this divine perspective, our thoughts, attitudes, and actions are transformed.

We begin to perceive the world through the lens of the Kingdom, where limitations give way to possibilities, and earthly constraints are replaced by heavenly abundance.

Comparing the limitations of a worldly or carnal way of thinking to the expansiveness of a Kingdom mindset reveals a striking contrast. Like the person standing next to the Empire State Building, those who operate with a worldly perspective can only see the towering height and imposing presence of their circumstances. Their vision is confined, and they struggle to grasp the vastness of God's plans for their lives.

However, when we adopt the mind of Christ, our perception transcends these confines. It is as if we are lifted into the skies, viewing life from an airplane where the once monumental structure appears small and insignificant against the backdrop of the vast expanse. Kingdom thinking allows us to see the bigger picture, where the challenges that once appeared insurmountable become manageable, and the burdens that once weighed us down are lifted.

From this heavenly vantage point, we gain a new understanding, a divine wisdom that enables us to navigate through life's twists and turns with grace and purpose. The mind of Christ shapes our thoughts, aligning them with God's truth and renewing our minds to think as He thinks. Our attitudes are transformed, as we embrace humility, love, and forgiveness, reflecting the character of our heavenly King. ****And our actions flow naturally from this Kingdom thinking, as we walk in complete surrender to the king of kings.

Jesus is the King of kings, and as such it is not that we are as the old bracelet said, "what would Jesus do?" (WWJD), it is more about what is he actually doing? The Kingdom way of thinking, actually grants us the opportunity to let heaven think on our behalf. For some that may seem undesirable, but once one understands that heaven never fails, and that God will never allow his word to return unto Him unfulfilled, then they will begin to prosper in ways that they never could've imagined.

When we view life through a carnal mentality, everything around us appears larger than life, overwhelming us with our own smallness. We become consumed by our limitations and insecurities, unable to see beyond our own inadequacies.

But when we shift our perspective and take our seat in heavenly places in Christ Jesus, a remarkable transformation occurs. We begin to see the world as Christ sees it, not through the lens of our own limitations, but through the lens of His greatness and power. It is no longer about who we are or are not, but about who He is and how magnificent He is.

From this elevated position, we realize that the challenges and obstacles that once loomed large are but fleeting moments in the grand tapestry of God's plan. We recognize that our struggles are merely opportunities for His strength to be made perfect in our weakness. And we understand that the greatness of our God far surpasses anything we could ever face.

So, let us embrace the mind of Christ, allowing it to shape our thinking, attitudes, and actions. Let us rise above the limitations of a carnal mentality and soar into the heights of Kingdom thinking. For it is in this sacred space that we discover the fullness of who we are in Christ and the boundless possibilities that lie before us.

As we walk in the truth that we are seated in heavenly places with Christ Jesus, let us view life through His eyes, knowing that nothing is too big for Him. May we find solace in the fact that our smallness is magnified by His greatness, and that we are more than conquerors through Him who loves us.

So, let us go forth, armed with the mind of Christ, and face the challenges of life with unwavering faith and confidence. For in Him, we have the power to overcome, to rise above, and to see everything as Christ sees it—through the lens of His unfathomable greatness.

Kingdom Meditations:

Philippians 2:4-7 New Century Version (NCV)
In your lives you must think and act like Christ Jesus. Christ himself was like God in everything. But he did not think that being equal with God was something to be used for his own benefit. But he gave up his place with God and made himself nothing.

Chapter 5: Cultivating a Kingdom Mindset: Unveiling the Power Within

Imagine a radio, with its unmistakable on/off switch. For believers, faith operates just like that switch. When we have faith, we are turned on to hear the messages of heaven, much like a radio receiving a clear signal. However, there are moments when the signal becomes fuzzy, and that's when we need to fine-tune our reception by adjusting the radio dial.

In the realm of Kingdom thinking, spiritual disciplines such as prayer, meditation, and fasting play a crucial role. They act as the hands that gently adjust the dial, ensuring that we can hear the heavenly messages with utmost clarity. Prayer connects us directly to the divine, allowing us to seek guidance, express our gratitude, and align our hearts with God's will. Meditation helps us quiet the noise within, enabling us to hear the whispers of heaven amidst the chaos of life. And fasting, this intentional act of self-denial, purifies our spirits and sharpens our spiritual senses, enabling us to tune in to the frequencies of heaven.

Just as adjusting the radio dial requires patience and attentiveness, cultivating a Kingdom mindset through spiritual disciplines demands our commitment and dedication. It is through these practices that we fine-tune our hearts and minds, aligning ourselves with the divine frequency of truth, wisdom, and love.

Much like a radio signal, the heavenly messages are constantly being transmitted. However, without the proper adjustment, we risk missing out on the profound revelations and guidance that God desires to impart to us. It is through the intentional practice of spiritual disciplines that we ensure our hearts and minds are receptive and attuned to the heavenly frequency.

Just as a radio allows us to hear music, news, and various broadcasts, cultivating a Kingdom mindset through spiritual disciplines allows us to hear the voice of God clearly. As we engage in prayer, meditation, and fasting, we adjust our dial, fine-tuning our reception to receive divine wisdom, direction, and comfort.

Let us not underestimate the power of these spiritual disciplines. They are not mere rituals or obligations but rather vital tools that enable us to connect with God and enhance our understanding of His Kingdom. Through prayer, meditation, and fasting, we cultivate a mindset that aligns our thoughts, desires, and actions with God's truth, love, and purpose.

So, let us be intentional in our pursuit of a Kingdom mindset. Let us embrace the power within us, the power to adjust our spiritual dial and tune in to the heavenly frequencies. As we engage in fasting, prayer, and even giving of alms to the poor, let us remember that these are all means to grow in the Spirit-led life. However, they all share a common requirement - the unwavering belief in the power and presence of God.

In the Gospel of Mark, we are reminded of the profound truth that lies at the core of Kingdom thinking: "ONLY BELIEVE." It is through our belief, our unshakable faith, that we unleash the full potential of these spiritual disciplines. Fasting, prayer, and giving become transformative acts when we approach them with hearts full of belief, trusting in the power and goodness of God.

So, as we embark on this journey of cultivating a Kingdom mindset, let us not underestimate the power of belief. Let us fix our eyes on the One who holds all power and authority, and let our belief in Him guide us in every step we take. May our fasting, prayer, biblical study and even our acts of giving be rooted in this unwavering belief, allowing us to experience the fullness of the Spirit-led life.

As we cultivate a Kingdom mindset, may we be reminded that it is through belief that we access the incredible power within us. Let us embrace these spiritual disciplines as tools to deepen our faith, align our hearts with God's will, and unveil the power of the Kingdom in our lives. Only believe, and watch as the transformative power of God's Spirit manifests in extraordinary ways.

Kingdom Meditations:

1. Romans 6:18 (NIV): "You have been set free from sin and have become slaves to righteousness."

2. Romans 12:2 (NIV): "Do not conform to the pattern of this world, but be transformed by the renewing of your mind. Then you will be able to test and approve what God's will is—his good, pleasing and perfect will."

3. Galatians 5:1 (NIV): "It is for freedom that Christ has set us free. Stand firm, then, and do not let yourselves be burdened again by a yoke of slavery."

4. 2 Corinthians 10:5 (NIV): "We demolish arguments and every pretension that sets itself up against the knowledge of God, and we take captive every thought to make it obedient to Christ."

5. Ephesians 4:22-24 (NIV): "You were taught, with regard to your former way of life, to put off your old self, which is being corrupted by its deceitful desires; to be made new in the attitude of your minds; and to put on the new self, created to be like God in true righteousness and holiness."

Chapter 6: Overcoming the Pull of the World: Resisting the Works of the Flesh

In the annals of history, one poignant example of the power of mindset can be found in the struggle of many African Americans after their liberation from the shackles of slavery. The physical chains may have been broken, but their minds remained ensnared by the remnants of their past. The journey to true freedom required more than just emancipation; it demanded a complete renewal of their thinking, a transformation to function effectively in the Dominion of Being Free.

Similarly, in the realm of Kingdom thinking, believers are called to rise above the temptations and enticements of the world. We are beckoned to resist the works of the flesh and embrace the liberating power of the Kingdom. Just as many African Americans faced the challenge of adjusting to freedom, we too must confront the shackles that restrict our lives.

The works of the flesh, those deceitful desires that entice us, seek to keep us bound to a life of mediocrity and worldly indulgence. They whisper promises of temporary satisfaction, leading us astray from the path of righteousness. However, Kingdom thinking teaches us to recognize these empty allurements and to overcome their pull.

To resist the works of the flesh, we must first recognize the power of our thoughts. Like many African Americans who needed their minds renewed to function effectively in freedom, we too must undergo a transformative process. It is a process that begins with the belief in the power of Kingdom thinking, the belief that we are not bound by the limitations of the world, but rather, we are citizens of a higher realm.

As we embrace Kingdom thinking, we understand that the battle against the works of the flesh is not fought solely on the external battlefield. It is a battle that takes place within the recesses of our minds, where negative thoughts and worldly desires attempt to gain a foothold. But with the power of Kingdom thinking, we can resist their influence and break free from their grasp.

Now is the time to shed the shackles of negative thinking and embrace the freedom that Kingdom thinking offers. Let us learn from the struggles and triumphs of those who have gone before us, understanding that just as African Americans were emancipated from slavery, Christ has emancipated us from the bondage of sin.

Through His sacrifice, Christ not only broke the chains of sin that held us captive, but He also bestowed upon us the Holy Spirit, the divine force that empowers us to renew our minds. This Spirit fills us with a knowledge of Christ, enabling us to discern between the works of the flesh and the ways of the Kingdom.

In the depths of our being, the Spirit works tirelessly to transform our thinking, aligning it with the truth and righteousness of the Kingdom. As we yield to His guidance, our minds are renewed, and we begin to see the world through the lens of God's perspective.

No longer slaves to the temptations and allurements of the world, we are now citizens of the Kingdom, called to walk in the freedom and dominion that Christ has bestowed upon us. With each step we take, guided by Kingdom thinking, we resist the works of the flesh and embrace a life of righteousness, love, and purpose.

Let us, therefore, embrace the power of Kingdom thinking, allowing it to permeate every aspect of our lives. May we be strengthened by the understanding that through Christ, we have been set free not only from the bondage of sin but also from the limitations of negative thinking.

In the forthcoming Book 2: The Power of Kingdom Thinking - Breaking the Chains of the Works of the Flesh, we will delve deeper into the strategies and principles that enable us to walk victoriously in the Kingdom.

The story of Americans' emancipation of slaves serves as a powerful example of the transformative power of freedom. Just as they had to overcome the physical chains that bound them, so too are we called to break free from the bondage of sin and man's religion.

Through the sacrifice of Christ, we have been not only emancipated from the consequences of sin but also given the Holy Spirit to renew our minds. This Spirit guides us in discerning the ways of the world and empowers us to resist the works of the flesh.

By embracing Kingdom thinking, we align our thoughts with the truth and righteousness of the Kingdom. We become aware of the deceitful allurements that seek to hold us captive and instead choose a life of righteousness, love, and purpose.

Let us embrace the power of Kingdom thinking and allow it to permeate every aspect of our lives. As we walk in the freedom and dominion that Christ has bestowed upon us, we can overcome the pull of the world and experience the fullness of life in the Kingdom of God. May our renewed minds be a testament to the liberating and transformative power of Christ's love and grace.

Kingdom Meditations:

1. Matthew 6:33: "Make seeking God's kingdom and righteousness your top priority, and all these things will be given to you as well."

2. Philippians 4:8: "Finally, my brothers and sisters, think about whatever is true, noble, right, pure, lovely, admirable, excellent, or praiseworthy."

3. Colossians 3:2 : "Set your minds on things above, not on earthly things."

4. Romans 12:2 : "Do not conform to the pattern of this world, but let God transform you by renewing your mind. Then you will know what God wants you to do, and you will agree that what he wants is excellent and good."

Chapter 7: Reigniting the Power of Kingdom Thinking: Reconnecting with God's Design

In order to reignite the power of Kingdom Thinking and reconnect with God's original design, it is vital that we first turn our attention to the foundational scripture found in Genesis 1:26. Within this profound passage, we discover the essence of dominion and the role it plays in our understanding of Kingdom Thinking.

"And God said, 'Let us make mankind in our image, in our likeness, so that they may rule over the fish in the sea and the birds in the sky, over the livestock and all the wild animals, and over all the creatures that move along the ground.'"

These words, spoken by the Creator Himself, unveil a divine plan for humanity. To comprehend the true meaning of dominion, we must delve deeper into its essence and purpose.

At its core, dominion can be defined as the authority and power granted by God to mankind. It encompasses the responsibility to influence and rule over the various aspects of creation. However, it is crucial to note that this dominion does not extend to the rule over other human beings. Instead, it is a call to steward and govern the natural world in alignment with God's intentions.

God's intention in granting humanity dominion was not to establish a hierarchical system of control, but rather to invite us into a partnership with Him in the unfolding of His creation. It is within this framework that Kingdom Thinking takes root.

As we explore the depths of Kingdom Thinking, we come to realize that it is not just a mindset or a way of thinking, but a paradigm that encompasses our entire existence. It is a profound understanding that we are co-creators with God, entrusted with the responsibility to influence and shape the world around us.

However, the narrative of dominion takes a different turn as we examine the course of human history. Despite being created to be influenced and ruled by God from heaven, mankind has often rejected His divine rule. This rejection is not a matter of superiority or defiance, but rather a consequence of our inherent human nature.

This rejection is beautifully depicted in Psalm 2, where we are given insights into the rebellion and resistance against God's authority. The psalmist speaks of the nations and their futile attempts to cast off God's rule, highlighting the inherent desire within humanity to assert their independence and pursue their own agendas.

In this regard, Psalm 2 serves as a poignant reminder of the consequences of turning away from God's design for dominion. It reveals the inherent struggle within of humanity to assert their own dominion, often leading to chaos, brokenness, and a disconnection from God's intended purpose.

However, despite humanity's failure to fully embrace and walk in the true essence of dominion, God's original design still stands. The invitation to participate in His divine plan remains open to all. It is within this context that Kingdom Thinking becomes crucial.

To reignite the power of Kingdom Thinking, we must shift our focus from self-centered desires and ambitions to aligning ourselves with God's purposes and intentions. It requires a surrendering of our own agendas and a realignment of our thoughts and actions with the principles of God's Kingdom. It is about recognizing that true dominion is not about exerting control over others, but about stewarding and nurturing the world around us in a way that reflects God's love, justice, and righteousness.

As we reconnect with God's design for dominion, we begin to see the transformative power it holds. It is not just about taking charge or asserting authority, but about becoming instruments of God's grace, mercy, and restoration. It is about using our influence and power to bring about positive change, to uplift and empower others, and to cultivate an environment where God's Kingdom can manifest in all its glory.

Reigniting the power of Kingdom Thinking requires a conscious effort to renew our minds and align our thoughts with God's truth. It means seeking His wisdom, guidance, and understanding, and allowing His Spirit to transform us from within. It means embracing the call to be ambassadors of His Kingdom, bringing His light and love into every sphere of influence.

Dominion, as defined in Genesis 1:26, is the authority and power granted by God to humanity to influence and rule over the natural world. True dominion is about stewarding and nurturing creation in alignment with God's intentions. Kingdom Thinking encompasses this understanding and calls us to realign our thoughts, actions, and priorities with God's Kingdom principles. It is through embracing and living out this mindset that we can reignite the power of Kingdom Thinking and reconnect with God's original design for humanity.

Kingdom Meditation:

1. Genesis 1:26-28 - "Then God said, 'Let us make mankind in our image, in our likeness, so that they may rule over the fish in the sea and the birds in the sky, over the livestock and all the wild animals, and over all the creatures that move along the ground.' So God created mankind in his own image, in the image of God he created them; male and female he created them. God blessed them and said to them, 'Be fruitful and increase in number; fill the earth and subdue it. Rule over the fish in the sea and the birds in the sky and over every living creature that moves on the ground.'"

2. Psalm 2:1-4 - "Why do the nations conspire and the peoples plot in vain? The kings of the earth rise up and the rulers band together against the Lord and against his anointed, saying, 'Let us break their chains and throw off their shackles.' The One enthroned in heaven laughs; the Lord scoffs at them."

3. Matthew 6:10 - "Your kingdom come, your will be done, on earth as it is in heaven."

4. Romans 12:2 - "Do not conform to the pattern of this world, but be transformed by the renewing of your mind. Then you will be able to test and approve what God's will is—his good, pleasing and perfect will."

5. Colossians 3:2 - "Set your minds on things above, not on earthly

things."

6. 2 Corinthians 5:20 - "We are therefore Christ's ambassadors, as though God were making his appeal through us. We implore you on Christ's behalf: Be reconciled to God."

Chapter 8. Breaking Free from the Bondage of Limited Thinking:

In chapter 6 we discussed that we have overcome slave bondage through the finished work of Christ. In this chapter, we will delve deeper into the concept of inferiority complexes and their profound impact on our lives as believers in the Kingdom of God. To fully embrace the power of Kingdom living, it is crucial that we confront and overcome these limiting beliefs and thought patterns that hinder us from experiencing the abundant life that God has destined for us.

What is slavery? Slavery, in its essence, is the dominion and ownership of one person upon another. It is a system born out of the belief that one individual is superior to another, and therefore, has the right to exert control and authority over them. While the physical chains of slavery may have been broken, the remnants of this oppressive mindset continue to linger within our society.

Many descendants of slaves still bear the burden of an inferiority complex, a deep-seated belief that they are somehow inherently inferior to others. These narratives of inferiority have been interwoven into the very fabric of our society, subtly seeping into our consciousness and shaping our perceptions of ourselves and others. Whether it is the color of our skin, the texture of our hair, or the features we possess, these societal constructs have created a distorted lens through which we view ourselves.

But as believers in the Kingdom of God, we must recognize the truth of our identity. We are sons and daughters of the Most High God, created in His image and called to walk in His authority. Our worth and value are not determined by societal standards or the opinions of others. Rather, they are rooted in our divine heritage as heirs to the Kingdom.

Inferiority complexes limit our lives as believers in multiple ways. Firstly, they hinder us from fully embracing and walking in the authority that God has given us. When we perceive ourselves as inferior, we undermine our own ability to exercise the power and influence that comes with our Kingdom citizenship. We shrink back from taking bold steps of faith and stepping into the purposes and plans that God has for us.

Secondly, inferiority complexes rob us of the joy and freedom that are inherent in Kingdom living. They imprison us within the confines of self-doubt and self-criticism, preventing us from fully embracing and enjoying the abundant life that Jesus promised. Instead of walking in confidence and boldness, we find ourselves shackled by insecurity and fear.

But there is hope. The power of Kingdom thinking enables us to break free from the bondage of limited thinking, including the chains of inferiority complexes. We must renew our minds with the truth of God's Word and allow His Spirit to transform us from the inside out. It is essential that we align our thoughts with the truth of who we are in Christ.

God's heart towards us, His children, is one of love, acceptance, and affirmation. He sees us as fearfully and wonderfully made, beautifully crafted with unique gifts and talents. He desires for us to walk in the fullness of our identity as His sons and daughters, to embrace our worth and value in Him.

Therefore, it is crucial that we repent of any thoughts that hinder us from living in the truth of who we truly are in Him. We must confront and challenge the lies of inferiority that have held us captive for far too long. By surrendering these limited beliefs and thought patterns at the foot of the cross, we open ourselves up to the transformative power of God's truth and love.

As we embrace our true identity as children of the Kingdom, we can step into the fullness of Kingdom living. We can walk in boldness, confidence, and authority, knowing that we are loved, accepted, and cherished by our Heavenly Father. No longer bound by the chains of inferiority, we can experience the abundant life that God has prepared for us.

In conclusion, breaking free from the bondage of limited thinking, including inferiority complexes, is a vital step in unlocking the power of Kingdom living. We are called to challenge and confront these beliefs that hinder us from fully embracing our true identity in Christ. Let us repent of any thoughts that hinder us from living in the truth of who we truly are in Him and allow God's transformative love and truth to renew our minds. As we do so, we will experience the fullness of Kingdom living and walk in the authority and abundance that God has destined for us as His beloved children.

Kingdom Meditation:

1. Genesis 1:27 - "So God created man in his own image, in the image of God he created him; male and female he created them."

2. Galatians 3:26 - "So in Christ Jesus you are all children of God through faith."

3. Ephesians 2:10 - "For we are God's handiwork, created in Christ Jesus to do good works, which God prepared in advance for us to do."

4. Romans 8:17 - "Now if we are children, then we are heirs—heirs of God and co-heirs with Christ, if indeed we share in his

sufferings in order that we may also share in his glory."

5. 2 Corinthians 5:17 - "Therefore, if anyone is in Christ, the new creation has come: The old has gone, the new is here!"

Chapter 9: Walking in Kingdom Authority: Unlocking the Power Within

As believers, we have been chosen to represent the King of kings in this world. We are more than mere followers; we are ambassadors of Christ, entrusted with the task of expressing His nature and demonstrating His power in the earth. Our lives should serve as a reflection of the potential that lies within us when we yield to the mind of Christ.

When we examine the life of Jesus, we witness a multitude of ways in which He displayed the power of His Father and expressed His Father's attributes. Through healing the sick, speaking to storms, walking on water, multiplying fish and loaves, and even raising the dead, Jesus revealed the heart and power of His Father. These miraculous acts were not mere displays of supernatural abilities, but rather deliberate demonstrations of the authority and dominion that come from being a citizen of the Kingdom.

Just as an ambassador represents not themselves but rather their country of origin, we too represent a heavenly kingdom. Our citizenship lies in heaven, and like any other ambassador, we are fully supported and backed by our King and His Kingdom.

This divine backing gives us the authority and power to exercise Kingdom principles in our daily lives.

Walking in Kingdom authority requires an understanding of our identity as ambassadors of Christ. We must recognize that we have been commissioned by the King Himself to carry out His will on earth. This understanding grants us the confidence and boldness to operate in the same power and authority that Jesus demonstrated during His time on earth.

Moreover, as ambassadors, we are not left to navigate this world on our own. We have been given the Holy Spirit as our guide and companion. It is through the Holy Spirit that we are empowered to walk in Kingdom authority, unlocking the power within us. He equips us with supernatural wisdom, discernment, and spiritual gifts that enable us to represent the Kingdom with excellence and effectiveness.

To walk in Kingdom authority, we must also align our thoughts and actions with the principles of the Kingdom. Our minds must be renewed by the Word of God, as it is through the knowledge and understanding of His truth that we gain access to the abundant life and authority He has promised us. By meditating on His Word and submitting our thoughts and desires to His will, we position ourselves to operate in the fullness of Kingdom authority.

As we walk in Kingdom authority, we become agents of transformation in the world around us. Our lives bear witness to the reality of a Kingdom that is not of this world, a Kingdom marked by love, power and righteousness. This begs the question: Are we truly walking as ambassadors of Christ, representing His Kingdom, or are we merely followers of man's religion?

Let us examine our lives and evaluate the extent to which we are expressing the nature and power of our King. Are we boldly demonstrating His attributes and authority in our daily interactions, or are we conforming to the standards and expectations of this world? Are we walking in Kingdom authority, unlocking the power within us, or are we settling for a lukewarm existence?

May this chapter serve as a wake-up call, urging us to step out of the shadows of complacency and into the light of Kingdom authority. Let us embrace our role as ambassadors of Christ, yielding to the mind of our King and allowing His power to flow through us. Only then can we truly make a lasting impact on this world and fulfill our divine purpose.

So, I ask you, dear reader: Are you walking as a true ambassador of Christ, or are you content with being a mere follower of man's religion? The choice is yours to make, and the power to walk in

Kingdom authority lies within you.

Kingdom Meditation:

1. Matthew 28:18-20 - "And Jesus came and said to them, 'All authority in heaven and on earth has been given to me. Go therefore and make disciples of all nations, baptizing them in the name of the Father and of the Son and of the Holy Spirit, teaching them to observe all that I have commanded you. And behold, I am with you always, to the end of the age.'"

2. Luke 10:19 - "Behold, I have given you authority to tread on serpents and scorpions, and over all the power of the enemy, and nothing shall hurt you."

3. Acts 1:8 - "But you will receive power when the Holy Spirit has come upon you, and you will be my witnesses in Jerusalem and in all Judea and Samaria, and to the end of the earth."

4. Ephesians 2:6-7 - "And raised us up with him and seated us with him in the heavenly places in Christ Jesus, so that in the coming ages he might show the immeasurable riches of his grace in kindness toward us in Christ Jesus."

5. 2 Corinthians 5:20 - "Therefore, we are ambassadors for Christ, God making his appeal through us. We implore you on behalf of Christ, be reconciled to God."

6. Colossians 3:17 - "And whatever you do, in word or deed, do everything in the name of the Lord Jesus, giving thanks to God the Father through him."

Chapter 10: The Renewed Mind: Embracing the Reality of Kingdom Thinking

In this transformative chapter, we delve into the significance and practicalities of renewing our minds to align with Kingdom thinking. By doing so, we not only experience a change in our lifestyles and attitudes but also tap into the true power of repentance.

Matthew 3:2 declares, "Repent, for the kingdom of heaven is at hand." But what exactly does this mean? It goes beyond a simple call to confess our sins, although that is undoubtedly crucial. Jesus, in uttering these words, was unveiling a greater way to live. He was introducing heaven's way of thinking, bringing forth a new paradigm for humanity.

Jesus, the Logos, the very embodiment of Heaven's logic and thought, came in the form of flesh to display the mind of the Father. His arrival was not just a mere event; it was a revelation of a new mindset, a divine perspective that had the power to transform lives. Repentance, therefore, is not limited to remorse for sins committed, but it is akin to a spiritual brain surgery, where our old ways of thinking are replaced with the mind of

Christ.

When we truly embrace repentance, our minds undergo a radical transformation. It is the process through which the person we were becomes the person we were always meant to be. As scripture reminds us, "For as a man thinks in his heart, so is he." (Proverbs 23:7) Our thoughts shape our reality, and when our thoughts align with Christ, our lives begin to reflect His nature.

The true focus of repentance is Christ Himself. It is not merely about turning away from sin, but rather turning towards Him. As we turn our gaze upon Christ, our hearts are captivated, and our minds are renewed. It is in this renewal that we find our true identity and purpose. Our thoughts, desires, and actions are transformed by the power of the Kingdom. We begin to think like citizens of the Kingdom, viewing ourselves and the world through the lens of eternity.

The journey of renewing our minds is not a one-time event but a continuous process. It is a lifelong commitment to align our thoughts with the thoughts of God. It requires discipline, surrender, and a willingness to let go of our own limited understanding. In doing so, we open ourselves up to the limitless possibilities of Kingdom thinking.

Practicalities of renewing our minds involve immersing ourselves in God's Word, allowing it to shape our thoughts and renew our minds. The Bible serves as our guide, providing us with the wisdom and truth needed to navigate the complexities of life through a Kingdom perspective.

In addition to studying Scripture, prayer becomes a vital tool in the process of renewing our minds. Through prayer, we communicate with God, seeking His guidance and surrendering our thoughts and desires to Him. It is in this intimate connection with our Heavenly Father that we receive the necessary insight and revelation to align our thinking with His.

Furthermore, surrounding ourselves with a community of believers who share in the pursuit of Kingdom thinking is essential. Iron sharpens iron, and in the company of like-minded individuals, we can encourage and challenge one another to continually renew our minds. Together, we can grow in our understanding of God's truth and experience the transformation that comes from Kingdom thinking.

As we embrace the reality of Kingdom thinking and allow our minds to be renewed, we will witness a profound change in our lifestyles and attitudes. The old patterns of thinking and behaving will give way to a new way of living. Our actions will reflect the character of Christ, and our interactions with others will be marked by love, grace, and compassion.

In conclusion, the power of repentance lies in the renewal of our minds. It is not a mere confession of sins but a transformative journey towards embracing Kingdom thinking. As we align our thoughts with the mind of Christ, we discover our true identity and purpose. Through the study of Scripture, prayer, and fellowship with other believers, we continually renew our minds and experience the profound impact of Kingdom thinking in our lives. Let us embark on this journey of repentance and embrace the reality of Kingdom thinking, for it is in this transformation that we find true fulfillment and abundant life.

Kingdom Meditations:

1. Romans 12:2 - "Do not conform to the pattern of this world, but be transformed by the renewing of your mind. Then you will be able to test and approve what God's will is—his good, pleasing and perfect will."

2. Ephesians 4:23-24 - "Instead, let the Spirit renew your thoughts and attitudes. Put on your new nature, created to be like God— truly righteous and holy."

3. Philippians 2:5 - "You must have the same attitude that Christ Jesus had."

4. Colossians 3:2 - "Set your minds on things above, not on earthly things."

5. 1 Corinthians 2:16 - "For, 'Who can know the Lord's thoughts? Who knows enough to teach him?' But we understand these things, for we have the mind of Christ."

6. 2 Corinthians 10:5 - "We demolish arguments and every pretension that sets itself up against the knowledge of God, and we take captive every thought to make it obedient to Christ."

7. Proverbs 23:7 - "For as he thinks in his heart, so is he."

Chapter 11: Living Above Circumstances: The Power of a Renewed Perspective

In the midst of my travels, I once encountered a sight that stirred within me a deep sense of sadness and reflection. Along the side of the road, I beheld an eagle, its once glorious wings now broken and battered. The national bird, a symbol of power and majesty, was reduced to a state of vulnerability and helplessness.

As I gazed upon this wounded creature, a profound realization dawned upon me. In a way, this eagle mirrored the condition of humanity following the fall of Adam. Just as this majestic bird had its wings broken, so too were we, as descendants of Adam, left broken and separated from the fullness of our potential.

However, my heart was filled with hope, for I knew that there was a restorative power at work. Just as the eagle's wings could be healed, so too could our spiritual wings be restored through the redemptive work of Christ. His grace and mercy became the wind beneath our wings, enabling us to rise above the storms of life and soar to new heights.

You see, the eagle's wings are not merely physical appendages;

they represent something far greater. They symbolize the grace and mercy bestowed upon us by our Heavenly Father. Adam, in his pristine state, possessed these divine gifts, allowing him to dwell in perfect harmony with God. However, with the fall of mankind, a distorted and counterfeit version of grace and mercy was introduced, hindering us from reaching our true potential.

But here lies the power of kingdom thinking - the ability to tap into the true essence of our spiritual wings. It is through the understanding and application of God's grace and mercy that we can victoriously navigate through any circumstance that comes our way. By embracing a renewed perspective rooted in the Kingdom, we can display the manifold wisdom of God in our lives.

Just as the eagle uses its wings to rise above the storms that threaten its existence, we too can harness the power of grace and mercy to transcend the challenges that surround us. When we adopt a kingdom mindset, we recognize that our circumstances do not define us. Instead, we are defined by the limitless possibilities and divine purpose that God has placed within us.

Like the eagle, we are called to soar above the storms of life, to display the beauty and wisdom of our Creator. The power of kingdom thinking empowers us to utilize our spiritual wings - grace and mercy - to rise above every trial and tribulation. In doing so, we become living testimonies of the transformative power of God's Kingdom. We showcase His goodness, His faithfulness, and His ability to turn brokenness into restoration.

As we embrace the power of kingdom thinking, Remember these words, Kingdom thinking enables us to rise above challenging circumstances and maintain a perspective rooted in God's truth. It is in life's trials and tribulations that we have the opportunity to display the greatness of our God. Just as the eagle soars above the storms, so can we, for we are empowered by the grace and mercy of our Heavenly Father.

Let us, then, take hold of this renewed perspective, allowing the wings of grace and mercy to carry us to new heights. No matter what storms may come our way, we can rise above, knowing that our identity is rooted in the Kingdom of God.

May you be inspired to live above circumstances, to embrace the power of a renewed perspective, and to soar with the strength and grace of an eagle. For in doing so, you will manifest the true power of kingdom thinking and exemplify the abundant life that God has destined for you.

Kingdom Meditation:

1. Isaiah 40:31 (NIV) - "But those who hope in the LORD will renew

their strength. They will soar on wings like eagles; they will run and not grow weary, they will walk and not be faint."

2. Romans 12:2 (NIV) - "Do not conform to the pattern of this world, but be transformed by the renewing of your mind. Then you will be able to test and approve what God's will is—his good, pleasing and perfect will."

3. 2 Corinthians 4:18 (NIV) - "So we fix our eyes not on what is seen, but on what is unseen, since what is seen is temporary, but what is unseen is eternal."

4. Philippians 4:8 (NIV) - "Finally, brothers and sisters, whatever is true, whatever is noble, whatever is right, whatever is pure, whatever is lovely, whatever is admirable—if anything is excellent or praiseworthy—think about such things."

Chapter 12: The Kingdom Revelation: The Disruptive Power of Kingdom Thinking

Kingdom thinking at its core is very disruptive. Its impact on individuals and communities is profound, as it brings about transformation and influences others. Just as Christ's way of living interrupted the flow of the world, His very presence became a disruptive force, interfering with the kingdom of darkness.

The essence of Kingdom thinking lies in the power of light to interrupt darkness. No matter how deep the darkness engulfing individuals or communities, the presence of Christ would bring a disruptive interruption. This truth was vividly manifested in the encounter between Jesus and the man possessed by a legion of demons.

This demonized man resided in a region consumed by darkness, but when Jesus approached, His light shone upon the man, causing the demons to flee. They were forced to jump into a herd of swine, thereby disrupting the economy of the region. The consumption of swine was forbidden according to the law of Moses, thus highlighting the unraveling of sin's grasp through the very presence of Kingdom thinking.

Furthermore, the disciples themselves walked in the power of Kingdom thinking. Their lives were deeply influenced and transformed as they embraced the teachings and presence of Christ. This truth is evident in the story recounted in Acts 16:16-21.

In this passage, we witness the apostle Paul and his companions encountering a slave girl who possessed a spirit of divination. This girl had the ability to predict the future and brought her owners a great deal of profit. However, as the disciples walked in the authority of the Kingdom, they recognized the presence of darkness within her.

With Kingdom thinking guiding their actions, Paul commanded the spirit to leave the girl in the name of Jesus Christ. Instantly, the spirit departed, liberating the girl from its oppressive hold. While this act of deliverance brought freedom to the girl, it also disrupted the financial gain of her owners, leading to their anger and subsequent persecution of Paul and Silas.

Through this story, we witness the power of Kingdom thinking in action. It not only transforms individual lives but also disrupts the norms and systems of the world. Just as Christ's presence disrupted the economy of the region by casting out demons, the disciples' adherence to Kingdom thinking shattered the bondage of the slave girl and challenged the exploitative practices of her owners.

The lesson here is clear: Kingdom thinking brings about radical transformation, both personally and communally. The power of Kingdom thinking is not limited to the past but is available to us today. As we embrace this transformative mindset, we have the potential to bring about profound change in our own lives and the communities around us. Just as Christ's presence disrupted darkness and the disciples walked in the authority of the Kingdom, we too can be agents of transformation.

Now, let us pause and reflect upon our own lives. Are we truly embracing Kingdom thinking? Are we allowing the light of Christ to interrupt the darkness within us and in the world around us? Are we willing to disrupt the status quo and challenge the systems of sin and injustice?

May we have the courage to embrace Kingdom thinking, knowing that it has the power to transform lives and communities. Let us be the disruptive force that brings about positive change, standing firm in the authority and truth of God's Kingdom. May our lives be a testament to the transformative power of Kingdom thinking, bringing light and hope to a world in need.

Kingdom Meditation:

1. Luke 8:26-39 (The healing of the demon-possessed man)
"Heal the sick who are there and tell them, 'The kingdom of God has come near to you.'" (Luke 10:9)

2. Acts 16:16-21 (The deliverance of the slave girl)
"She kept following Paul and us, shouting, 'These men are servants of the Most High God, who are proclaiming to you the way of salvation.'" (Acts 16:17)

3. Matthew 5:14-16 (Being the light of the world)
"You are the light of the world. A town built on a hill cannot be hidden. Neither do people light a lamp and put it under a bowl. Instead, they put it on its stand, and it gives light to everyone in the house. In the same way, let your light shine before others, that they may see your good deeds and glorify your Father in heaven."

4. Matthew 6:33 (Seeking God's Kingdom)
"But seek first his kingdom and his righteousness, and all these things will be given to you as well."

5. Romans 12:2 (Transformed by the renewing of our minds)
"Do not conform to the pattern of this world, but be transformed by the renewing of your mind. Then you will be able to test and approve what God's will is—his good, pleasing and perfect will."

6. Matthew 28:19-20 (The Great Commission)

"Therefore go and make disciples of all nations, baptizing them in the name of the Father and of the Son and of the Holy Spirit, and teaching them to obey everything I have commanded you. And surely I am with you always, to the very end of the age."

Chapter 13: Fulfilling Your Kingdom Purpose: Experiencing the Abundance of God's Kingdom

In life we often find ourselves searching for meaning and purpose. We yearn for something that goes beyond the mundane, something that transcends the temporal and touches the eternal. In this pursuit, we may stumble upon Matthew 6:33, a verse that holds within it the key to unlocking the abundant life that God desires for us.

"Seek first the kingdom of God and his righteousness, and all these things will be added to you." These words, spoken by Jesus Himself, reveal a profound truth about the way we are meant to live. They beckon us to a life where our purpose aligns with God's divine plan, where our footsteps are guided by His sovereign hand.

So, what does it mean to seek the kingdom of God? The word "kingdom" in this verse denotes not a geographical location, but rather the rule and reign of God. It invites us to actively pursue the authority and sovereignty of Christ in our lives. This pursuit, however, must not be detached from our pursuit of righteousness – being in right standing with God.

We must never underestimate the interconnectedness of seeking the rule of God and pursuing righteousness. For it is in this delicate balance that we find the gateway to experiencing the abundance of God's kingdom. When we wholeheartedly seek after the kingdom, all power, provision, protection, purpose, and potential are lavishly poured out upon us. Why? Because we align ourselves with the principles and values of the kingdom of Heaven, and we embrace the role of Christ in our lives.

Imagine a river flowing through a parched land. As the water courses through the dry soil, it brings life, refreshment, and nourishment to everything in its path. Similarly, when we seek the rule of God and pursue righteousness, we position ourselves to receive the unending flow of the abundance of His kingdom. This abundance is not merely material possessions or worldly success, but rather a deep and profound satisfaction that transcends earthly measures.

To fulfill our unique kingdom purposes, we must first understand that our purpose is intricately woven into the grand tapestry of God's plan for His creation. We are not random accidents or aimless wanderers. No, we are divinely crafted beings, endowed with gifts, talents, and passions for a specific purpose – to bring glory to God and advance His kingdom on earth.

When we embrace this truth and commit ourselves to seeking after the kingdom of God, we align ourselves with the mind of Christ. We begin to see the world through His eyes, to love as He loves, and to serve as He serves. Our actions become infused with purpose, our decisions guided by wisdom, and our words empowered by truth.

As we walk in the authority of the kingdom, we become catalysts for transformation. Our lives become a testament to the power of God at work within us, drawing others to the light of His love. We become agents of change, bringing healing to brokenness, restoration to the weary, and hope to the hopeless.

The journey of restoring the mind of Christ is not without challenges. We will face opposition, doubt, and moments of weakness. But in those moments, we can anchor ourselves in the truth that God is faithful. He has equipped us with the Holy Spirit, who empowers us to overcome every obstacle and walk in victory.

So, as Book 1 of this series comes to a close, I urge you to embrace the power of kingdom thinking. Seek the rule of God and pursue righteousness with unwavering faith. Embrace your unique kingdom purpose and live it out with passion and conviction. Allow the mind of Christ to shape your thoughts, words, and actions, and watch as the abundance of God's kingdom unfolds before you.

Remember, this is just the beginning of a three-part journey. There is more to discover, more to learn, and more to experience as we delve deeper into the power of kingdom thinking. But for now, let us rejoice in the transformation that has taken place within us and anticipate the incredible adventures that lie ahead.

May the mind of Christ be fully restored in us, and may His kingdom come and His will be done on earth as it is in Heaven. Amen.

Check out these other books by

Eric T. Williams on Amazon:

Overcoming Nothos: Victory of fatherlessness and the spirit of bastard

https://a.co/d/9FNy9ym

Tools of the Trade: 22-day Meditation of the Elementary Doctrines of the Christian Faith

https://a.co/d/6q3DFwT

Decoding Melchizedek: A 30-Day Meditation

https://a.co/d/fWLqPGh

The Seed of Righteousness: Cultivating A Life of Righteousness by Faith

https://a.co/d/ijwioum

Notes

Notes

Notes

Notes

Notes

Notes

Notes

Notes

Notes

Notes

Notes

Notes

Notes

Notes

Notes

Notes

Notes

Notes

Notes

Made in the USA
Columbia, SC
31 March 2024

33458929R00048